Charles Darwin
Quotes... Vol.11
by The Secret Libraries

Paperback EDITION

The Secret Libraries

Published by The Secret Libraries
www.thesecretlibraries.com
Annotation and Artists Background by The Secret Libraries 2016

All rights reserved.

No part of this publication may be reproduced, stored in a retrieval system or transmitted in any form or by any means, electronic, mechanical, photocopying or otherwise without the prior permission of The Secret Libraries.

Paperback:
ISBN-13: 978-1540607768
ISBN-10: 1540607763

Copyright © 2016

Quotes...

This book provides a selected collection of 146 quotes by Charles Darwin.

Charles Darwin

1809-1882

A man who dares to waste one hour of time has not discovered the value of life.

> It is not the strongest of the species that survives, not the most intelligent that survives. It is the one that is the most adaptable to change.

> **There is** no fundamental difference between man and animals in their ability to feel pleasure and pain, happiness, and misery.

> If the misery of the poor be caused not by the laws of nature, but by our institutions, great is our sin.

❝

The love for all living creatures is the most noble attribute of man.

❞

" **I am not** apt to follow blindly the lead of other men. "

❝

If I had my life to live over again, I would make it a rule to read some poetry, listen to some music, and see some painting or drawing at least once a week, for perhaps the part of my brain now atrophied would then have been kept alive through life. The loss of these tastes is a loss of happiness.

❞

> **To suppose** that the eye with all its inimitable contrivances for adjusting the focus to different distances, for admitting different amounts of light, and for the correction of spherical and chromatic aberration, could have been formed by natural selection, seems, I confess, absurd in the highest degree...The difficulty of believing that a perfect and complex eye could be formed by natural selection, though insuperable by our imagination, should not be considered subversive of the theory.

❝

It is always advisable to perceive clearly our ignorance.

❞

> **The mystery** of the beginning of all things is insoluble by us; and I for one must be content to remain an agnostic.

> We are not here concerned with hopes or fears, only with truth as far as our reason permits us to discover it.

> **If it could** be demonstrated that any complex organ existed, which could not possibly have been formed by numerous, successive, slight modifications, my theory would absolutely break down. But I can find no such case.

> The highest possible stage in moral culture is when we recognise that we ought to control our thoughts.

> **We stopped** looking for monsters under our bed when we realized that they were inside us.

❝

An American monkey, after getting drunk on brandy, would never touch it again, and thus is much wiser than most men.

❞

Intelligence is based on how efficient a species became at doing the things they need to survive.

❝
I am not the least afraid to die.
❞

Blushing is the most peculiar and most human of all expressions.

> **We must, however,** acknowledge, as it seems to me, that man with all his noble qualities... still bears in his bodily frame the indelible stamp of his lowly origin.

> One general law, leading to the advancement of all organic beings, namely, multiply, vary, let the strongest live and the weakest die.

> **Ignorance** more frequently begets confidence than does knowledge: it is those who know little, not those who know much, who so positively assert that this or that problem will never be solved by science.

❝

The power to charm the female has sometimes been more important than the power to conquer other males in battle.

❞

> **Besides love** and sympathy, animals exhibit other qualities connected with the social instincts which in us would be called moral.

> **With savages**, the weak in body or mind are soon eliminated; and those that survive commonly exhibit a vigorous state of health. We civilised men, on the other hand, do our utmost to check the process of elimination; we build asylums for the imbecile, the maimed, and the sick; we institute poor-laws; and our medical men exert their utmost skill to save the life of every one to the last moment.

The surgeon may harden himself whilst performing an operation, for he knows that he is acting for the good of his patient; but if we were intentionally to neglect the weak and helpless, it could only be for a contingent benefit, with a certain and great present evil. Hence we must bear without complaining the undoubtedly bad effects of the weak surviving and propagating their kind;

> **We can** allow satellites, planets, suns, universe, nay whole systems of universe, to be governed by laws, but the smallest insect, we wish to be created at once by special act.

"

As man advances in civilization, and small tribes are united into larger communities, the simplest reason would tell each individual that he ought to extend his social instincts and sympathies to all members of the same nation, though personally unknown to him. This point being once reached, there is only an artificial barrier to prevent his sympathies extending to the men of all nations and races.

"

> I am quite conscious that my speculations run quite beyond the bounds of true science.

> Great is the power of steady misrepresentation.

❞

Nothing is easier than to admit in words the truth of the universal struggle for life, or more difficult--at least I have found it so--than constantly to bear this conclusion in mind.

❞

❝

Man selects only for his own good: Nature only for that of the being which she tends.

❞

" **I see no** good reasons why the views given in this volume should shock the religious views of anyone. "

> Freedom of thought is best promoted by the gradual illumination of men's minds which follows from the advance of science.

> Those who look tenderly at the slave owner, and with a cold heart at the slave, never seem to put themselves into the position of the latter; what a cheerless prospect, with not even a hope of change! picture to yourself the chance, ever hanging over you, of your wife and your little children — those objects which nature urges even the slave to call his own — being torn from you and sold like beasts to the first bidder! And these deeds are done and palliated by men, who profess to love their neighbours as themselves, who believe in God, and pray that his Will be done on earth! It makes one's blood boil, yet heart tremble, to think that we Englishmen and our American descendants, with their boastful cry of liberty, have been and are so guilty...

❝

...for the shield may be as important for victory, as the sword or spear.

❞

> The loss of these tastes [for poetry and music] is a loss of happiness, and may possibly be injurious to the intellect, and more probably to the moral character, by enfeebling the emotional part of our nature.

> To kill an error is as good a service as, and sometimes even better than, the establishing of a new truth or fact.

...I feel most deeply that the whole subject is too profound for the human intellect. A dog might as well speculate on the mind of Newton. Let each man hope & believe what he can.

> **For my own** part I would as soon be descended from that heroic little monkey, who braved his dreaded enemy in order to save the life of his keeper; or from that old baboon, who, descending from the mountains, carried away in triumph his young comrade from a crowd of astonished dogs—as from a savage who delights to torture his enemies, offers up bloody sacrifices, practices infanticide without remorse, treats his wives like slaves, knows no decency, and is haunted by the grossest superstitions.

False facts are highly injurious to the progress of science, for they often endure long; but false views, if supported by some evidence, do little harm, for everyone takes a salutary pleasure in proving their falseness; and when this is done, one path towards error is closed and the road to truth is often at the same time opened.

❝

There is grandeur in this view of life, with its several powers, having been originally breathed by the Creator into a few forms or into one; and that, whilst this planet has gone cycling on according to the fixed law of gravity, from so simple a beginning endless forms most beautiful and most wonderful have been and are being evolved.

❞

> The question of whether there exists a Creator and Ruler of the Universe has been answered in the affirmative by some of the highest intellects that have ever existed.

❝

A scientific man ought to have no wishes, no affections, - a mere heart of stone.

❞

> **Wherever** the European had trod, death seemed to pursue the aboriginal.

"

The more civilised so-called Caucasian races have beaten the Turkish hollow in the struggle for existence. Looking to the world at no very distant date, what an endless number of the lower races will have been eliminated by the higher civilized races throughout the world.

"

> Each living creature must be looked at as a microcosm--a little universe, formed of a host of self-propagating organisms, inconceivably minute and as numerous as the stars in heaven.

Nevertheless so profound is our ignorance, and so high our presumption, that we marvel when we hear of the extinction of an organic being.

> We are always slow in admitting any great change of which we do not see the intermediate steps.

> The very essence of instinct is that it's followed independently of reason.

> Natural Selection almost inevitably causes much extinction of the less improved forms of life and induces what I have called Divergence of Character.

“

Nothing is easier than to admit in words the truth of the universal struggle for life, or more difficult - at least I have found it so - than constantly to bear this conclusion in mind...We behold the face of nature bright with gladness...We do not see, or we forget, that the birds which are idly singing round us mostly live on insects and seeds, and are thus constantly destroying life.

”

> He who understands baboons would do more towards metaphysics than Locke.

> We will now discuss in a little more detail the Struggle for Existence.

"One day, on tearing off some old bark, I saw two rare beetles, and seized one in each hand. Then I saw a third and new kind, which I could not bear to lose, so I popped the one which I held in my right hand into my mouth. Alas! it ejected some intensely acrid fluid, which burnt my tongue so that I was forced to spit the beetle out, which was lost, as was the third one."

> But Natural Selection, as we shall hereafter see, is a power incessantly ready for action, and is immeasurably superior to man's feeble efforts, as the works of Nature are to those of Art.

In conclusion, it appears that nothing can be more improving to a young naturalist, than a journey in distant countries.

Only picture to yourself a nice soft wife on a sofa with good fire, & books & music.

> Often a cold shudder has run through me, and I have asked myself whether I may have not devoted myself to a fantasy.

> **But then** with me the horrid doubt always arises whether the convictions of man's mind, which has been developed from the mind of the lower animals, are of any value or at all trustworthy. Would any one trust in the convictions of a monkey's mind, if there are any convictions in such a mind?

> A fair result can be obtained only by fully stating and balancing the facts and arguments on both sides of each question.

> But then arises the doubt, can the mind of man, which has, as I fully believe been developed from a mind as low as that possessed by the lowest animal, be trusted when it draws such grand conclusions?

I think it inevitably follows, that as new species in the course of time are formed through natural selection, others will become rarer and rarer, and finally extinct. The forms which stand in closest competition with those undergoing modification and improvement will naturally suffer most.

> As natural selection acts by competition, it adapts the inhabitants of each country only in relation to the degree of perfection of their associates; so that we need feel no surprise at the inhabitants of any one country, although on the ordinary view supposed to have been specially created and adapted for that country, being beaten and supplanted by the naturalised productions from another land.

"

When we no longer look at an organic being as a savage looks at a ship, as at something wholly beyond his comprehension; when we regard every production of nature as one which has had a history; when we contemplate every complex structure and instinct as the summing up of many contrivances, each useful to the possessor, nearly in the same way as when we look at any great mechanical invention as the summing up of the labour, the experience, the reason, and even the blunders of numerous workmen; when we thus view each organic being, how far more interesting, I speak from experience, will the study of natural history become!

"

> **As buds give rise** by growth to fresh buds, and these, if vigorous, branch out and overtop on all sides many a feebler branch, so by generation I believe it has been with the great Tree of Life, which fills with its dead and broken branches the crust of the earth, and covers the surface with its ever-branching and beautiful ramifications.

“

One hand has surely worked throughout the universe.

”

> **A grain in** the balance will determine which individual shall live and which shall die - which variety or species shall increase in number, and which shall decrease, or finally become extinct.

I have always maintained that, excepting fools, men did not differ much in intellect, only in zeal and hard work; and I still think there is an eminently important difference.

It is difficult to believe in the dreadful but quiet war lurking just below the serene facade of nature.

> Englishmen rarely cry, except under the pressure of the acutest grief; whereas in some parts of the Continent the men shed tears much more readily and freely.

> But a plant on the edge of a desert is said to struggle for life against the drought, though more properly it should be said to be dependent upon the moisture.

❝

From the strong principle of inheritance, any selected variety will tend to propagate its new and modified form.

❞

> **Such simple** instincts as bees making a beehive could be sufficient to overthrow my whole theory.

It is necessary to look forward to a harvest, however distant that may be, when some fruit will be reaped, some good effected.

> What wretched doings come from the ardor of fame; the love of truth alone would never make one man attack another bitterly.

> The limit of man's knowledge in any subject possesses a high interest which is perhaps increased by its close neighbourhood to the realms of imagination.

> The expression often used by Mr. Herbert Spencer of the Survival of the Fittest is more accurate, and is sometimes equally convenient.

"
Our descent, then, is the origin of our evil passions!!
The devil under form of Baboon is our grandfather.
"

> The earthquake, however, must be to every one a most impressive event: the earth, considered from our earliest childhood as the type of solidity, has oscillated like a thin crust beneath our feet; and in seeing the laboured works of man in a moment overthrown, we feel the insignificance of his boasted power.

> I have stated, that in the thirteen species of ground-finches, a nearly perfect gradation may be traced, from a beak extraordinarily thick, to one so fine, that it may be compared to that of a warbler.

> **Look at** a plant in the midst of its range! Why does it not double or quadruple its numbers? We know that it can perfectly well withstand a little more heat or cold, dampness or dryness, for elsewhere it ranges into slightly hotter or colder, damper or drier districts. In this case we can clearly see that if we wish in imagination to give the plant the power of increasing in numbers, we should have to give it some advantage.

> **I am fully** convinced that species are not immutable; but that those belonging to what are called the same genera are lineal descendants of some other and generally extinct species, in the same manner as the acknowledged varieties of any one species are the descendants of that species.

The mind is a chaos of delight, out of which a world of future & more quiet pleasure will arise.

❝

Rain does not fall in order to make the corn grow,
any more than it falls to spoil the farmer's corn when threshed out of doors...

❞

"So what hinders the different parts (of the body) from having this merely accidental relation in nature? as the teeth, for example, grow by necessity, the front ones sharp, adapted for dividing, and the grinders flat, and serviceable for masticating the food; since they were not made for the sake of this, but it was the result of accident. And in like manner as to other parts in which there appears to exist an adaptation to an end. Wheresoever, therefore, all things together (that is all the parts of one whole) happened like as if they were made for the sake of something, these were preserved, having been appropriately constituted by an internal spontaneity; and whatsoever things were not thus constituted, perished and still perish." We here see the principle of natural selection shadowed forth, but how little Aristotle fully comprehended the principle, is shown by his remarks on the formation of the teeth.), the first author who in modern times has treated it in a scientific spirit was Buffon. But as his opinions fluctuated greatly at different periods, and as he does not enter on the causes or means of the transformation of species, I need not here enter on details.

"

But when on shore, & wandering in the sublime forests, surrounded by views more gorgeous than even Claude ever imagined, I enjoy a delight which none but those who have experienced it can understand - If it is to be done, it must be by studying Humboldt.

"

> How odd it is that anyone should not see that all observation must be for or against some view if it is to be of any service!

> **My books** have sold largely in England, have been translated into many languages, and passed through several editions in foreign countries. I have heard it said that the success of a work abroad is the best test of its enduring value. I doubt whether this is at all trustworthy; but judged by this standard my name ought to last for a few years.

> In regard to the amount of difference between the races, we must make some allowance for our nice powers of discrimination gained by a long habit of observing ourselves.

> I could show fight on natural selection having done and doing more for the progress of civilization than you seem inclined to admit. Remember what risk the naticns of Europe ran, not so many centuries ago of being overwhelmed by the Turks.

❝

One may say there is a force like a hundred thousand wedges...

❞

> But I am very poorly today & very stupid & I hate everybody & everything. One lives only to make blunders.

I had also, during many years, followed a golden rule, namely that whenever published fact, a new observation of thought came across me, which was opposed to my general results, to make a memorandum of it without fail and at once; for I had found by experience that such facts and thoughts were far more apt to escape from the memory than favourable ones.

> In the distant future I see open fields for far more important researches. Psychology will be based on a new foundation, that of the necessary acquirement of each mental power and capacity by gradation.

A grand and almost untrodden field of inquiry will be opened, on the causes and laws of variation, on correlation of growth, on the effects of use and disuse, on the direct actions of external conditions, and so forth.

Sexual selection acts in a less rigorous manner than natural selection. The latter produces its effects by the life or death at all ages of the more or less successful individuals.

> **The great variability** of all the external differences between the races of man, likewise indicates that they cannot be of much importance; for if important, they would long ago have been either fixed and preserved, or eliminated.

> I have deeply regretted that I did not proceed far enough at least to understand something of the great leading principles of mathematics, for men thus endowed seem to have an extra sense.

> I do not believe, as we shall presently see, that all our dogs have descended from any one wild species; but, in the case of some other domestic races, there is presumptive, or even strong, evidence in favour of this view.

> ... **I fell asleep** on the grass, and awoke with a chorus of birds singing around me, and squirrels running up the trees, and some woodpeckers laughing, and it was as pleasant and rural a scene as I ever saw, and I did not care one penny how any of the beasts or birds had been formed.

> Two distinct elements are included under the term "inheritance"— the transmission, and the development of characters.

It is a fact of some importance to us, that peculiarities appearing in the males of our domestic breeds are often transmitted, either exclusively or in a much greater degree, to the males alone.

> Or she may accept, as appearances would sometimes lead us to believe, not the male which is the most attractive to her, but the one which is the least distasteful.

" It is no valid objection that science as yet throws no light on the far higher problem of the essence or origin of life. Who can explain what is the essence of the attraction of gravity? "

> **I am convinced** that natural selection has been the main but not exclusive means of modification.

> Alexander von Humboldt was the greatest scientific traveller who ever lived.

>

Reason tells me of the extreme difficulty or rather impossibility of conceiving this immense and wonderful universe, including man with his capability of looking far backwards and far into futurity, as the result of blind chance or necessity. When thus reflecting I feel compelled to look to a First Cause having an intelligent mind in some degree analogous to that of man; and I deserve to be called a Theist.

"

> When I view all beings not as special creations, but as the lineal descendants of some few beings which lived long before the first bed of the Cambrian system was deposited, they seem to me to become ennobled.

> He [Erasmus Darwin] used to say that 'unitarianism was a feather-bed to catch a falling Christian.

> Man in his arrogance thinks himself a great work, worthy of the interposition of a deity. More humble, and I believe truer, to consider him created from animals.

❝

I fully agree with all that you say on the advantages of H. Spencer's excellent expression of 'the survival of the fittest.'

❞

> I have called this principle, by which each slight variation, if useful, is preserved, by the term natural selection, in order to mark its relation to man's power of selection.

Sympathy

beyond the confines of man, that is humanity to the lower animals, seems to be one of the latest moral acquisitions. It is apparently unfelt by savages, except towards their pets. How little the old Romans knew of it is shewn by their abhorrent gladiatorial exhibitions. The very idea of humanity, as far as I could observe, was new to most of the Gauchos of the Pampas. This virtue, one of the noblest with which man is endowed, seems to arise incidentally from our sympathies becoming more tender and more widely diffused, until they are extended to all sentient beings.

"

Although much remains obscure, and will long remain obscure, I can entertain no doubt, after the most deliberate study and dispassionate judgment of which I am capable, that the view which most naturalists entertain, and which I formerly entertained-- namely, that each species has been independently created--is erroneous.

"

> Let it also be borne in mind how infinitely complex and close-fitting are the mutual relations of all organic beings to each other and to their physical conditions of life; and consequently what infinitely varied diversities of structure might be of use to each being under changing conditions of life.

> Light will be thrown on the origin of man and his history.

"

My mind seems to have become a kind of machine for grinding general laws out of large collections of facts, but why this should have caused the atrophy of that part of the brain alone, on which the higher tastes depend, I cannot conceive.

"

❝

When a man merely speaks to, or just notices, his dog, we see the last vestige of these movements in a slight wag of the tail, without any other movement of the body, and without even the ears being lowered. Dogs also exhibit their affection by desiring to rub against their masters, and to be rubbed or patted by them.

❞

> **I am dying** by inches, from not having any body to talk to about insects...

> And thus, the forms of life throughout the universe become divided into groups subordinate to groups.

> I think an Agnostic would be the more correct description of my state of mind. The whole subject [of God] is beyond the scope of man's intellect.

"

... I had gradually come by this time, i.e., 1836 to 1839, to see that the Old Testament from its manifestly false history of the world, with the Tower of Babel, the rainbow at sign, &c., &c., and from its attributing to God the feelings of a revengeful tyrant, was no more to be trusted than the sacred books of the Hindoos, or the beliefs of any barbarian...

"

> ...large portions of the earth like wild-fire had some weight with me. Beautiful as is the morality of the New Testament, it can be hardly denied that its perfection depends in part on the interpretation which we now put on metaphors and allegories.

> **Natural selection** rendered evolution scientifically intelligible: it was this more than anything else which convinced professional biologists like Sir Joseph Hooker, T. H. Huxley and Ernst Haeckel.

This preservation of favourable individual differences and variations, and the destruction of those which are injurious, I have called Natural Selection, or the Survival of the Fittest.

If any man wants to gain a good opinion of his fellow men, he ought to do what I am doing: pester them with letters.

> It has already been stated that various parts in the same individual, which are exactly alike during an early embryonic period, become widely different and serve for widely different purposes in the adult state. So again it has been shown that generally the embryos of the most distinct species belonging to the same class are closely similar, but become, when fully developed, widely dissimilar.

How fleeting are the wishes and efforts of man! How short his time! Consequently how poor will his products be, compared with those accumulated by nature during whole geological periods. Can we wonder, then, that nature's productions should be far "truer" in character than man's productions; that they should be infinitely better adapted to the most complex conditions of life, and should plainly bear the stamp of far higher workmanship?

> It was evident that such facts as these, as well as many others, could only be explained on the supposition that species gradually become modified; and the subject haunted me.

> Since all organisms vary, and all reproduce themselves in greater numbers than can survive, there must always be competition between variants; in other words, the principle of natural selection, too, is universally applicable.

> It seems pretty clear that organic beings must be exposed during several generations to the new conditions of life to cause any appreciable amount of variation; and that when the organisation has once begun to vary, it generally continues to vary for many generations.

> **What a book** a devil's chaplain might write on the clumsy, wasteful, blundering, low, and horribly cruel work of nature!

> **This prophecy** has turned out entirely and miserably wrong.

> Hence if man goes on selecting, and thus augmenting, any peculiarity, he will almost certainly modify unintentionally other parts of the structure, owing to the mysterious laws of correlation.

> **Man could** no longer be regarded as the Lord of Creation, a being apart from the rest of nature. He was merely the representative of one among many Families of the order Primates in the class Mammalia.

> **I cannot** here give references and authorities for my several statements; and I must trust to the reader reposing some confidence in my accuracy.

❝

A pleasurable and excited state of mind, associated with affection, is exhibited by some dogs in a very peculiar manner, namely, by grinning.

❞

> We shall best understand the probable course of natural selection by taking the case of a country undergoing some physical change, for instance, of climate. The proportional numbers of its inhabitants would almost immediately undergo a change, and some species might become extinct.

> In all cases positive palaeontological evidence may be implicitly trusted; negative evidence is worthless, as experience has so often shown.

...But I own that I cannot see as plainly as others do, and as I should wish to do, evidence of design and beneficence on all sides of us. There seems to me too much misery in the world. I cannot persuade myself that a beneficent and omnipotent God would have designedly created the Ichneumonidæ with the express intention of their feeding within the living bodies of Caterpillars, or that a cat should play with mice.

> **The following** proposition seems to me in a high degree probable—namely, that any animal whatever, endowed with well-marked social instincts, the parental and filial affections being here included, would inevitably acquire a moral sense or conscience, as soon as its intellectual powers had become as well, or nearly as well developed, as in man. For, firstly, the social instincts lead an animal to take pleasure in the society of its fellows, to feel a certain amount of sympathy with them, and to perform various services for them.

Among the scenes which are deeply impressed on my mind, none exceed in sublimity the primeval forests undefaced by the hand of man; whether those of Brazil, where the powers of Life are predominant, or those of Tierra del Fuego, where Death and decay prevail. Both are temples filled with the varied productions of the God of Nature: -- no one can stand in these solitudes unmoved, and not feel that there is more in man than the mere breath of his body.

> At some future period, not very distant as measured by centuries, the civilised races of man will almost certainly exterminate and replace throughout the world the savage races. At the same time the anthropomorphous apes, as Professor Schaaffhausen has remarked, will no doubt be exterminated. The break will then be rendered wider, for it will intervene between man in a more civilised state as we may hope, than the Caucasian and some ape as low as a baboon, instead of as at present between the negro or Australian and the gorilla.

> But just in proportion as this process of extermination has acted on an enormous scale, so must the number of intermediate varieties, which have formerly existed, be truly enormous. Why then is not every geological formation and every stratum full of such intermediate links? Geology assuredly does not reveal any such finely graduated organic chain; and this, perhaps, is the most obvious and serious objection which can be urged against the theory. The explanation lies, as I believe, in the extreme imperfection of the geological record.

> Judging from the past, we may safely infer that not one living species will transmit its unaltered likeness to a distant futurity.

❝

He who believes that each being has been created as we now see it, must occasionally have felt surprise when he has met with an animal having habits and structure not at all in agreement.

❞

Charles Darwin
1809-1882

References & Further Reading
Works from Charles Darwin

Writings:

Extracts from Letters to Henslow
The Voyage of the Beagle
Zoology of the Voyage of H.M.S. Beagle
The Structure and Distribution of Coral Reefs
On the Tendency of Species to form Varieties; and on the Perpetuation of Varieties and Species by Natural Means of Selection
On the Origin of Species
Fertilisation of Orchids
Geological Observations on South America
Geological Observations on the Volcanic Islands
The Variation of Animals and Plants under Domestication
The Descent of Man, and Selection in Relation to Sex
The Expression of the Emotions in Man and Animals Insectivorous Plants
The Power of Movement in Plants
The Formation of Vegetable Mould through the Action of Worms
Autobiography
Correspondence
The Life and Letters of Charles Darwin
More Letters of Charles Darwin
List of described taxa

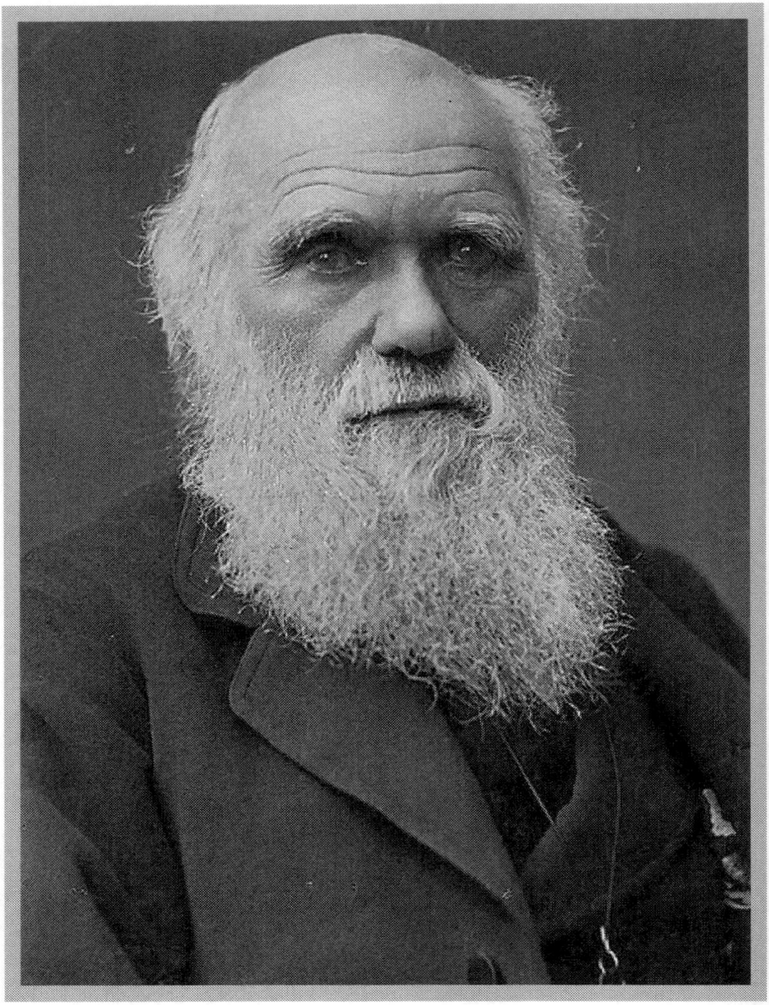

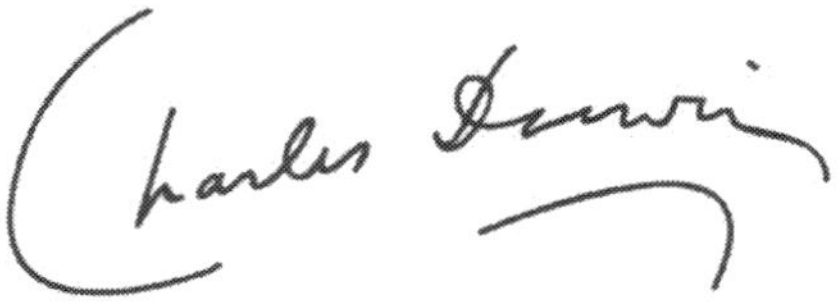
Charles Darwin

Quotes...

Receive a Kindle Edition in the series for FREE...

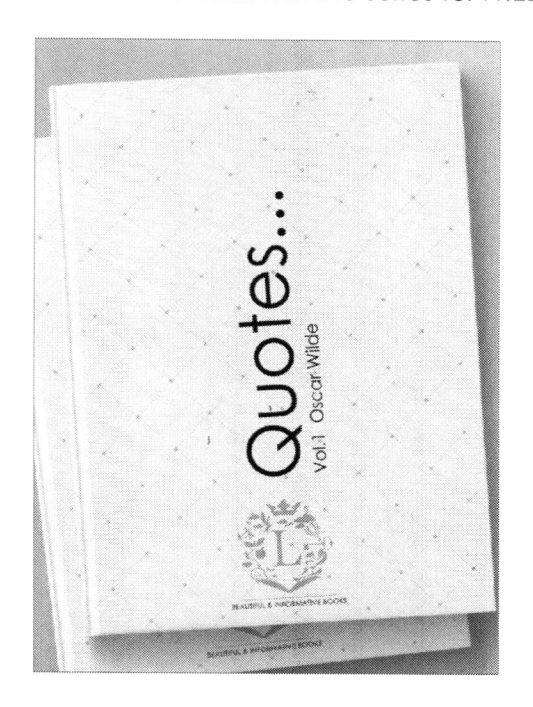

Sign up at
www.thesecretlibraries.com

Find us on:

The Secret Libraries

Published by The Secret Libraries
www.thesecretlibraries.com
Annotation and Artists Background by The Secret Libraries 2016

All rights reserved.

No part of this publication may be reproduced, stored in a retrieval system or transmitted in any form or by any means, electronic, mechanical, photocopying or otherwise without the prior permission of The Secret Libraries.

Paperback:
ISBN-13: 978-1540607768
ISBN-10: 1540607763

Copyright © 2016

For more information please find us at:

www.thesecretlibraries.com

Thank you for your purchase.

Printed in Great Britain
by Amazon